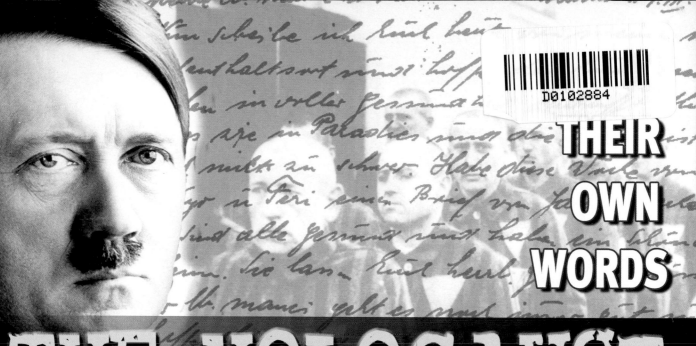

THEIR OWN WORDS

THE HOLOCAUST

A Primary Source History

Judy Bartel

GARETH**STEVENS**

GS

PUBLISHING

Cover photos:
Top: *Under the leadership of Adolf Hitler, Nazi Germany drove all of Europe into a catastrophic war and gave rise to one of the darkest periods in human history—the Holocaust.*
Bottom: *Few European Jews—not even children—were spared the systematic brutality of the Nazi camps.*

CONTENTS

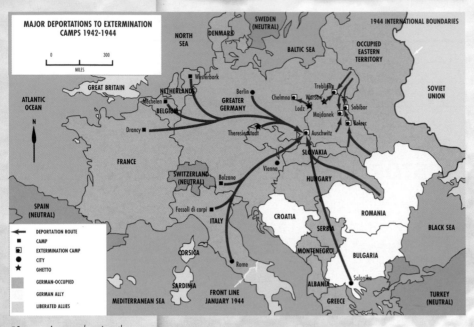

MAJOR DEPORTATIONS TO EXTERMINATION
CAMPS 1942-1944

0   300
MILES

1944 INTERNATIONAL BOUNDARIES

DEPORTATION ROUTE
CAMP
EXTERMINATION CAMP
CITY
GHETTO
GERMAN-OCCUPIED
GERMAN ALLY
LIBERATED ALLIES

FRONT LINE
JANUARY 1944

Above: A map showing the major extermination camps used during the Holocaust and the areas where the main deportations of the Jews took place.

B etween 1933 and 1945, six million Jews and countless others across Europe were persecuted and murdered systematically through a government-sponsored genocide. By 1945, two out of every three Jews on the continent had died from overwork, starvation, exposure to the elements, bullets, fire, poisonous gas, beatings, or hangings.

Every Jewish person living in Europe was a target for extermination by the Nazis. The perpetrators who carried out this massacre of the innocent were scientists, doctors, military and government personnel, and ordinary citizens. This frightening event became known as the Holocaust.

Below: A map showing the changing Nazi territory during World War II.

AXIS POWERS, AUGUST 1939
EXTENT OF AXIS CONTROL, MAY 1941
ALLIES
NEUTRAL NATIONS
AXIS OFFENSES
ALLIED OFFENSES
MAJOR BATTLES

After World War I, a defeated Germany fell into a social and economic depression. In the Treaty of Versailles, the victorious Allies had imposed a settlement upon the Germans that forced them to pay compensation and to take the blame for the war. Unemployment soared, inflation made the German currency worthless, and a new German government called the Weimar Republic was struggling to maintain democracy.

4

In 1919, Adolf Hitler, a corporal in the German army, was hired by the German military to spy on a political party called the German Workers' Party (later known as the Nazis). He became intrigued by the party's policies and eventually was invited to become its leader. Hitler was a powerful speaker, and through his dramatic speeches and theatrics, he managed to gain wide support for his party from the German public. The Nazis gained many seats in the Reichstag, the German Parliament, and in January 1933, Germany's president appointed Hitler chancellor, or leader, of Germany.

Above: *This photograph of Auschwitz was taken in 1991. Auschwitz was the largest concentration camp with a death total of 1.5 million. Once a person entered Auschwitz, the chances of leaving alive were very slim.*

Hitler and the Nazis' terrifying *Sturmabteilung* (SA) soldiers then used fear and violence to manipulate the German people and take complete control of the government. Hitler's protective police, the *Schutzstaffel* (SS), and the *Geheime Staatzpolizei* (GESTAPO) also silenced political opponents and others who spoke out against the Nazis. In March 1933, the first concentration camp for political dissenters opened at Dachau. Anyone who was identified as an opponent or enemy (communist, socialist, or trade union leader) was arrested, taken to a concentration camp, beaten, or

Right: *When Adolf Hitler came to power in Germany, he quickly unleashed a frightening campaign of persecution against the Jewish people of Europe.*

Below: *Stone statue in the garden of an old SS barracks. The barracks now serve as a museum.*

5

Above: *An emaciated survivor greets United States soldiers at the Buchenwald Concentration Camp on April 18, 1945.*

Below: *A postcard written by a Jewish prisoner at the Auschwitz-Birkenhau concentration camp. Most of these postcards were never delivered.*

even killed. Hitler was now in complete control. The Weimar Republic was dead.

Hitler had been a racist long before he became chancellor. He believed there existed a "master" race of physically fit, "racially pure" people called Aryans, and he saw this group as the future citizens of Germany and all of Europe. His plan to "purify" Germany became a major part of the Nazi plan. Hitler also believed it was critical to open up *lebensraum* (living space) for the Aryan people. To accomplish his goal, all people he deemed inferior had to be removed. German physicians were bound by law to sterilize anyone who was "inferior," including those who were mentally or physically disabled, bi-racial, or of ethnic minorities, such as the Gypsies, or Romani. These sterilizations were the Nazis' insurance that "inferior" people would not reproduce.

Hitler and other Nazi leaders considered the Jewish "race" in particular a danger to Germany's future. Thousands of years of anti-Semitism in Europe had created a history of prejudicial behavior toward Jews. Hitler's Nuremberg Race Laws defined Jewish people not as a religious group but as a race. Hitler claimed that the Jews were "parasites" who fed off of a "host" race and weakened it. The Jews, Hitler claimed, were responsible for all that ailed German society. As in the past, Jews became the scapegoat in Germany and other European countries.

The Nazis' prejudicial laws forbade Jews from owning businesses, practicing professions, and owning property. After the Germans invaded Poland in 1939, starting World War II, the Jews were forced from their homes into ghettos. Conditions in the ghettos were harsh. Several families lived in one room, with only the bare essentials to survive. Children could not got to school. All valuables had to be turned over to the Nazis. Many people died of disease and malnutrition. As the ghettos became overcrowded, Jews were transported by railroad cattle cars to concentration and, later, death camps.

As World War II progressed, the German army, called the Wehrmacht, marched across Europe. The Einsatzgruppen, or mobile killing squads, followed in the army's path, executing entire villages of Jews and either burying or burning the bodies in groups. Hitler was implementing his "Final Solution"— the extermination of the Jews. The Einsatzgruppen, however, were not the fastest nor most efficient way to murder, so the Nazis planned and built death camps. As the Allied troops closed in, the Nazis sent prisoners on "death marches" of several hundred miles, only to execute them upon their arrival at camps.

In January 1945, the first Soviet troops discovered the camps. Many prisoners were ill and continued to die after the camps were liberated. The survivors had the difficult and disheartening task of searching for loved ones. With homes, families, and livelihoods gone, many people spent years in displaced persons camps before attempting to resume their lives. This is the story of the Holocaust, a story that must be told and remembered so that such an atrocity can never be permitted to happen again.

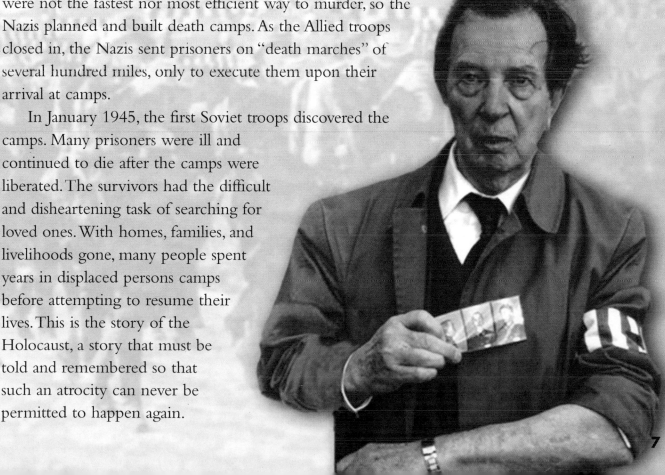

Left: *During Hitler's reign, the Jewish people were forced to wear the Star of David, shown here as a button, to identify themselves.*

Below: *An Auschwitz survivor holds up photos and shows the number tattooed on his arm. His armband is made from cloth cut from his prison uniform.*

Above: *A map of Europe after the Treaty of Versailles. Under its terms, Germany lost territory and suffered humiliation.*

Before World War I, Germany was the industrial powerhouse of Europe. The military was well-equipped with a strong land army and thriving navy. Germans held great pride in their writers, artists, and composers. The school system was world class, and most Germans received an excellent education. After the war, Germany had to pay war reparations, and its defeat caused resentment and bitterness that would undermine its new democracy.

"He had lost his leg on the battlefront, and he refused to try to use a wooden leg. Instead he rolled around the house in his wheelchair and stormed at the 'bureaucrats and bloodsuckers' who had brought Germany to disgrace. He described leaders of the civilian government as traitors, to whom we owe no loyalty or allegiance. When I brought home the black, red, and gold flag of the new republic (the old flag had been black, white and red), he ripped it up, spit on it, slapped me in the face and told me never to bring that rag into the house again."

Interview with the son of Johann Herbert, conducted in 1951 and later published in 1977.

THE GREAT WAR

On June 28, 1914, the heir to the Austro-Hungarian throne, Archduke Franz Ferdinand, and his wife were gunned down by a young Serbian terrorist. In response, Austria-Hungary declared war on Serbia. This declaration caused Russia, Serbia's ally, to mobilize against Austria-Hungary. Germany, an ally of Austria-Hungary, then declared war against Russia and invaded Belgium on a path toward France. Belgium's invasion brought its ally, Great Britain, into the conflict, and for four years the Great War (later known as World War I) raged across Europe.

The war ended in November 1918 with the defeat of Germany and

its allies. In the summer of 1919, the war's victors—Great Britain, France, Russia, and the United States—assembled at Versailles, France, to draw up a peace treaty. As part of the treaty's terms, Germany had to accept blame for the war and assume the war debts of countries that were destroyed. Initially Germany refused to sign the treaty, but it was told that

Right: *Kaiser Wilhelm II of Germany led his country into World War I.*

Below: *Despite Germany's air power—its Fokker Eindecker fighter planes were among the deadliest in the skies—the country was forced to surrender on November 11, 1918.*

TIME LINE
1914–1919

June 1914
Archduke Ferdinand assassinated.

July 1914
Germany pledges support to Austria-Hungary, which declares war on Serbia.

August 1914
The major European powers divide into two sides. Hitler joins the German army.

November 1918
Germany signs armistice and the war ends.

June 1919
Treaty of Versailles signed.

failure to sign would reignite war. The treaty's terms left Germany humiliated. Germany's defeat also spelled the end of its monarchy, and in January 1919, an era of democracy began. A democratic constitution was signed in the city of Weimar, establishing the Weimar Republic. The Weimar Republic, Germany's new government, would last until Adolf Hitler came to power.

HITLER'S ORIGINS

Adolf Hitler was born on April 20, 1889, in a small Austrian village. When Hitler's mother died when he was just 18, his life spun out of control. For several years he lived the life of a recluse in Vienna, where anti-Semitism was fashionable. There, Hitler developed a strong admiration for the city's anti-Semitic mayor, Karl Lueger. Hitler also developed strong, ruthless survival skills while living on the streets, and he became harsh, cynical, and anti-Semitic. In August 1914, Hitler joined the German army. When World War I ended, he was angered by the Germans' defeat. In 1919, Corporal Hitler was assigned to spy on an anti-Semitic, pro-military, nationalistic political party called the German Workers' Party. He became attracted, however, to the party's

Above: *The Hall of Mirrors at the Palace of Versailles, the room where the peace treaty was signed.*

"The Allied and Associated Governments affirm and Germany accepts the responsibility of Germany and her allies for causing all the loss and damage to which the Allied and Associated Governments and their nationals have been subjected as a consequence of the war imposed upon them by the aggression of Germany and her allies. The Allied and Associated Governments, however, require, and Germany undertakes, that she will make compensation for all damage done to the civilian population of the Allied and Associated Powers and to their property during the period of the belligerency of each as an Allied or Associated Power against Germany by such aggression by land, by sea and from the air, and in general all damage as defined in Annex l hereto."

Treaty of Versailles
PART VIII. REPARATION.
SECTION l. GENERAL PROVISIONS. ARTICLE 231.

Above: Map showing the Jewish population of Europe before the Holocaust.

Above: A photograph of Adolf Hitler as a young boy.

"Don't think that one can fight against disease without killing the cause, without exterminating the germ; and don't think that one can fight against racial tuberculosis without taking care that the peoples be freed of the germ of racial tuberculosis. The effect of Judaism will never disappear and the poisoning of the people will not end unless the cause—the Jews—are removed from our presence."

Adolf Hitler, Salzburg, August 7, 1920.

politics. He was discharged from the military and soon took control of the party. Hitler changed its name to the National Socialist German Workers' Party, or Nazi Party, in 1920. Under his leadership, the party flourished.

HITLER IN PRISON

In November 1923, the Nazis attempted to overthrow the German government by capturing several Bavarian officials. The attempt failed, however, and Hitler was caught, convicted of high treason, and sentenced to prison. During the nine months that he served, Hitler wrote out his plan for the future of Germany in his book *Mein Kampf* (*My Struggle*). In *Mein Kampf*, Hitler blamed the Weimar Republic, communists, and Jews for Germany's loss of World War I and the economic and social troubles that followed.

Right: A Polish Rabbi helps a Jewish student with lessons from the Hebrew bible. The boy was later murdered in one of Hitler's death camps.

Above: Hitler (far left, under the "X") fought in the Bavarian regiment of the German army during World War I.

September 1919
Hitler attends meeting of German Workers' Party.

Spring 1920
Party changes name and becomes popularly known as the Nazi Party. .

1923
Hitler becomes leader of the party. In November, the failed government overthrow takes place.

1924
Hitler sent to Landsberg prison for treason. He is released after just nine months.

1925
Hitler's *Mein Kampf* is published. The Schutzstaffel (SS)—Hitler's personal bodyguards—is formed.

1926
Hitler Jugend (Hitler Youth) is formed.

JEWS IN EUROPE

Jews had lived throughout Europe for over two thousand years. By the time Hitler came to power in 1933, nine million Jews were living in some twenty-one European countries. In eastern Europe, Jews mostly lived in small towns called shtetls. In these towns, most people spoke Yiddish, a mixture of German and Hebrew, and lived very traditional lives. Many wore traditional black caftans and were devoutly observant of the Jewish religion. In the large cities of western Europe, however, Jews lived side-by-side with non-Jews. Jews adopted the culture of their neighbors and friends, dressed and spoke the same, and worked in many different fields, including business, education, and the law.

Right: This racist German election poster from 1920 criticizes the idea of the "pure" Aryan marrying a Jew.

"Once, as I was strolling through the inner city, I suddenly encountered an apparition in a black caftan and black hair locks. Is this a Jew? was my first thought. For, to be sure, they had not looked like that in Linz. I observed the man furtively and cautiously, but the longer I stared at this foreign face, scrutinizing feature for feature, the more my first question assumed a new form: is this a German? . . . the more I saw, the more sharply they became distinguished in my eyes from the rest of humanity. . . . For me this was the time of the greatest spiritual upheaval I have ever had to go through. I had ceased to be a weak-kneed cosmopolitan and become an anti-Semite."

Adolf Hitler, *Mein Kampf*.

· DEVTSCHLAND ·

Above: *A 1933 election poster in Berlin urging citizens to vote for the joint ticket of Hitler and Hindenburg.*

Above: *A poster promoting the Hitler Youth movement. Membership eventually became compulsory.*

"I spoke for thirty minutes, and what before I had simply felt within me, without in any way knowing it, was now proved by reality: I could speak! After thirty minutes the people in the small room were electrified and the enthusiasm was first expressed by the fact that my appeal to the self-sacrifice of those present led to the donation of three hundred marks."

Adolf Hitler, *Mein Kampf.*

I n the 1930 election, the Nazis received more than 18 percent of the votes and catapulted from the smallest party in Germany to the second largest. In 1932, Hitler ran for president and lost by only 17 percent in a run-off vote. Despite the loss, Hitler was very popular. In January 1933, cabinet members badgered the ailing President Paul von Hindenburg into appointing Hitler chancellor of Germany. It was thought that by keeping him close, others could keep a watchful eye over the charismatic leader. Adolf Hitler, however, had been grossly underestimated.

THE RISE OF NAZI GERMANY

In 1929, the U.S. stock market crash caused Germany's economic problems to increase ten-fold. Businesses saw profits slip, and many companies went bankrupt. By 1932, the number of unemployed Germans had reached a record six million. Amazingly, the government actually raised taxes in the hopes of using the revenue to help the poor. The economic troubles made the weak Weimar Republic ripe for manipulation when Hitler was appointed chancellor. When the Reichstag building was set ablaze by an arsonist in February 1933, Hitler declared a national state of emergency. He convinced Hindenburg to declare the Decree of the Reich President for the Protection of People and State, which legalized mass arrests of socialists, communists, and any other Nazi opponents. Dachau, the first prison camp for political dissidents, opened in March 1933. Once his opponents were silenced, Hitler focused on the Jews.

Left: *German children in 1923 playing with money in the streets. Under the Weimar Republic, inflation was such that 1 U.S. dollar was worth 4.2 million Deutschmarks. German money was effectively worthless.*

Hitler became immersed in the German Workers' Party and even renamed it the National Socialist German Workers' Party, or Nazi Party for short. He also chose the symbol for the party, the swastika. What is now considered a symbol of hate, Hitler remembered as a decoration he had seen as a boy in the monastery where he had attended school:

"In the red we see the social idea of the movement, in the white the national idea, in the swastika the mission to struggle for the victory of Aryan man and at the same time the victory of the idea of creative work, which is eternally anti-Semitic and will always be anti-Semitic."

Adolf Hitler, *Mein Kampf.*

ANTI-SEMITISM

From 70 B.C., when the Roman Emperor Pompey the Great insisted that Jews worship Roman Gods, to present-day vandals drawing swastikas on the walls of a synagogue, anti-Semitism has had a long history.

Hatred of Jews grew after the death of Jesus in 33 A.D. Jews do not share the Christian belief that Jesus was the son of God. Although Jesus' death was ordered by the Romans, not the Jews, many Christians believe that the Jews were

TIME LINE
1933

January 30, 1933
Hitler appointed chancellor.

February 28, 1933
Nazis encourage an arsonist to burn Reichstag building. Emergency powers granted to Hitler.

March 22, 1933
Nazis open Dachau concentration camp near Munich, Germany.

March 23, 1933
German parliament passes Enabling Act giving Hitler dictatorial powers.

Above: *Adolf Hitler with President Paul von Hindenburg during ceremonies in Potsdam in March 1933, marking the reopening of the German parliament.*

"By appointing Hitler Chancellor of the Reich you have handed over our sacred German Fatherland to one of the greatest demagogues of all time. I prophesy to you this evil man will plunge our Reich into the abyss and will inflict immeasurable woe on our nation. Future generations will curse you in your grave for this action."

Telegram to Hindenburg from former General Erich Ludendorff

Above: *These two covers from official Hitler Youth magazines show Nazi expectations for what boys and girls should become. Girls' magazines told readers to work hard and look after German men, while boys' magazines emphasized adventure and excitement.*

"As a member of the storm troop of the NSDAP [Nazi Party] I pledge myself to its storm flag: to be always ready to stake life and limb in the struggle for the aims of the movement; to give absolute military obedience to my military superiors and leaders; to bear myself honorably in and out of service; to be always companionable towards other comrades."

A pledge taken by members of the *Sturmabteilung* (SA), the military wing of the Nazi Party.

responsible for his crucifixion, and some hold Jews collectively guilty for Jesus' death. Historically, this feeling has resulted in discriminatory laws against the Jews, particularly in the Christian regions of Europe. Forbidden to own land or

Below: *A Hitler Youth march taking place in 1938, before the outbreak of World War II.*

businesses across parts of the continent, some Jews became money lenders, leading to the stereotype that Jews are ruthless financiers. Hitler's anti-Semitic views attempted to convince non-Jewish people that the Jews were trying to dominate the world economically and politically. The fact that Jews were a minority— less than 1 percent of the German population—fueled Hitler's claims that they wielded power disproportionate to their small numbers.

HITLER YOUTH

Adolf Hitler's plan was to produce a military and social structure that would support his anti-Semitic ideology well into the future. To ensure loyalty for years to come, the Hitler *Jugend* (HJ or Hitler Youth), a boys' organization, was created. The

HJ grew in strength as the Nazi Party grew throughout the 1920s. In 1933, the HJ forcibly absorbed all other German children's organizations and had more than 3.5 million members, including boys ages thirteen to eighteen. School schedules were adjusted to include challenging physical fitness courses and courses that emphasized the Nazi themes of racial struggle and German pride. Courses such as biology were eventually removed from the curriculum. What had been a superb, world-class German school system became substandard almost overnight. Children were even encouraged to report family or neighbors who spoke out against the Nazi regime. Walter Hess, a Hitler Jugend, was elevated to the status of hero when he turned in his father for calling Hitler a crazed maniac. His father was taken to Dachau.

PERSECUTION OF THE JEWS

On March 23, 1933, the newly elected members of the Reichstag, the German parliament, met in Berlin. Now Nazi-dominated, the Reichstag passed the Enabling Act, a piece of legislation put forward by Hitler. Officially titled the Law for Removing the Distress of the People and the Reich, the Act effectively handed all power over to the chancellor, Hitler, and ended democracy in Germany. Just one week after the Act was passed, the Nazis organized a national boycott of Jewish shops and department stores.

Above: *A soldier models the uniform of the SA, also known as the Brownshirts, who helped enforce the boycott of Jewish shops.*

TIME LINE
1933

April 1
Nazis stage boycott of Jewish shops and businesses.

July 14
The Nazi Party is declared the only legal party in Germany. Jewish immigrants from Poland are stripped of their German citizenship.

GERMAN BOYS AND GIRLS!

"We National Socialists carried on our struggle for the sake of the German people and its future. The future of the people is its children—which is you. We thought about you as we fought, risking life and health and all we had to help the swastika to victory. You will be spared what the German people had to experience before 1933.

The fatherland's age of distress is past. The machines are running again, the chimneys are smoking. There is work and food. People are happy again and have found new faith. And all are working in the same direction. The people make up a great community, tied together a million-fold by common blood, and faces its future with heads held high.

You are our young team. You will take the storm flags from our hands and carry them into a happier future.

The doors of school are closing behind you. It has prepared you well. Be glad that the present day demands accomplishment and diligence of you. We Germans will not allow ourselves to be surpassed by any other people in the world. Join the ranks of creative Germans, build the new Reich, and be loyal to your last breath."

"You and Your People," from Reichswalter des NSLB (the Nazi organization for teachers), 1940.

Left: *The SA take books out of a Berlin library to burn them.*

Propaganda Minister Joseph Goebbels urged the boycott as a response to what he termed "anti-German atrocity propaganda" carried out by "international Jewry." The Nazis believed that the stories of Germany's atrocities during World War I were spread by newspapers that were "secretly controlled" by the Jews. The Nazis' military wing, the Sturmabteilung (SA or "Brownshirts"), stood in the doorways of Jewish-owned stores and encouraged Germans to "defend yourselves against the Jewish atrocity propaganda."

On May 10, 1933, students, accompanied by the SA, made heaping piles of books written by Jews or containing ideas deemed to

Above: *The Nuremberg Race Laws required Jews to identify themselves by wearing a Star of David badge. This one says* Jude, *meaning "Jew."*

be "unGerman." They poured gasoline on the books and set them ablaze. Authors like Albert Einstein, Sigmund Freud, and Ernest Hemingway, to name a few, were included in the inferno. Teachers were also under constant scrutiny by the

Above: *Works by writers and academics, including Sigmund Freud, the "father" of modern psychoanalytic theory, were banned by Hitler.*

"My program for educating youth is hard. Weakness must be hammered away. In my castles of the Teutonic Order a youth will grow up before which the world will tremble. I want a brutal, domineering, fearless, cruel youth. Youth must be all that. It must bear pain. There must be nothing weak and gentle about it. The free, splendid beast of prey must once again flash from its eye. . . . That is how I will eradicate thousands of years of human domestication. . . .That is how I will create the New Order."

Adolf Hitler, 1933.

"Restrictions on personal liberty, on the right of free expression of opinion, including freedom of the press; on the rights of assembly and association; and violations of the privacy of postal, telegraphic and telephonic communications and warrants for house searches, orders for confiscations as well as restrictions on property, are also permissible beyond the legal limits otherwise prescribed."

From the Decree of the Reich President for the Protection of People and State

Hitler Youth during lessons and faced mandatory background checks from Nazi officials to prove the "purity" of their genealogy. Teachers complained that the new education program did not give students the standard of education they had previously enjoyed, but that did not matter to the Nazis.

Below: *Joseph Goebbels was the Reich Minister for Public Enlightenment and Propaganda, which gave him total control over all of the German media and the arts.*

RACE LAWS

Although there are no defining physical or genetic characteristics of all Jews, Hitler claimed that Jews were a racially inferior group. The 1935 Nuremberg Race Laws revoked German citizenship of Jews, making it illegal for a Jewish person to marry or have sexual relations with a non-Jewish German. These laws also defined a "Jew" as a person who has three or four Jewish grandparents. The significance of these laws is that Judaism was now viewed as a race and not a religion. A person cannot change or renounce his or her race, so people who had converted from Judaism to Christianity, even priests and nuns, were now considered by law to be Jewish.

TIME LINE
1934–1938

August 2, 1934
German President Paul von Hindenburg dies. Hitler becomes *Führer* (leader).

September 15, 1935
Nuremberg Race Laws decreed.

March 12–13, 1938
Annexation of Austria.

July 1938
At Evian Conference in France the United States convenes a League of Nations conference with delegates from 32 countries to consider helping Jews fleeing Hitler. Results in inaction since no country will accept them.

July 25, 1938
Jewish doctors prohibited by law from practicing medicine.

October 5, 1938
Law requires Jewish passports to be stamped with a large red "J."

"The era of extreme Jewish intellectualism is now at an end. . . . The future German man will not just be a man of books, but a man of character. It is to this end that we want to educate you. As a young person, to already have the courage to face the pitiless glare, to overcome the fear of death, and to regain respect for death—this is the task of this young generation. And thus you do well in this midnight hour to commit to the flames the evil spirit of the past. This is a strong, great and symbolic deed—a deed which should document the following for the world to know: Here the intellectual foundation of the November [Democratic] Republic is sinking to the ground, but from this wreckage the phoenix of a new spirit will triumphantly rise."

Propaganda Minister Joseph Goebbels, Berlin 1933.

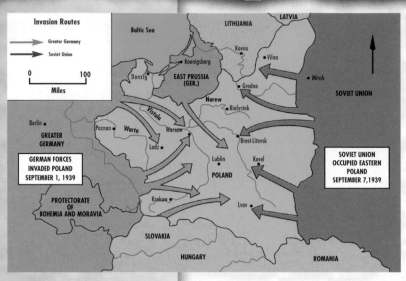

Above: A map showing the successful German invasion of Poland in September 1939.

On November 7, 1938, Ernst vom Rath, a German diplomat, was shot in the German Embassy in Paris by Herschel Grynszpan, a 17-year-old Polish Jewish refugee. Grynszpan had received a message that his family had been expelled from Germany and deported to a refugee camp on the Polish-German border. When vom Rath died two days later, the Nazis unleashed the largest campaign of violence against the German Jews up to this point.

Above: A Jewish shop owner in Berlin cleans up after Kristallnacht.

THE NIGHT OF BROKEN GLASS

Kristallnacht ("Night of Broken Glass") is the name given to the violent anti-Jewish action unleashed on German Jews on November 9, 1938. On this night 7,500 Jewish homes and businesses and 267 synagogues were vandalized or destroyed by fire. Over 30,000 Jews were taken to concentration camps, and 36 Jews were killed. Afterwards, despite the fact that Jews were the victims of this violence and destruction, the Jewish community was fined one million Reichsmarks. On November 12, 1938, a law was passed that prevented Jewish businesses from re-opening, placed a curfew on all Jews, and excluded Jews from many public places including schools. Newspapers around the world reported this violation of human

Below: Hitler forced all Jews to move into contained areas called ghettos, usually based in the poorest part of towns.

"The terrifying happenings of this ghoulish night, the Kristallnacht, are considered to be the prelude to the Holocaust. The SS began picking up Jewish families from their homes and were sending them to one of the numerous concentration camps that had sprung up like mushrooms all over Germany and Austria. But as Hitler had experienced in previous incidents, no world government lodged any serious condemnation strong enough to cause him concern."

From An Unbroken Chain, written by Holocaust survivor Henry Oertelt.

rights, yet no action was taken.

NAZIS MARCH ON

In the summer of 1938, thirty-two delegates from countries around the world, including the United States and Great Britain, joined Germany in Evian, France, to discuss the "Jewish problem." All countries showed disdain for Germany's treatment of Jews, yet they refused to relax their immigration policies so that Jews could leave Germany. The conference showed Hitler that other countries would not interfere with his plan to "cleanse" Germany of its Jews and open up *lebensraum* (living space for Aryans). His quest for more lebensraum influenced him to invade Poland in September 1939. Within weeks, the Polish army was defeated, and the Poles were at the mercy of the Nazi forces. The Nazis kidnapped Polish children who had Aryan features and sent them to be raised by Germans. Polish leaders were shot, and many Poles were relocated so German families could settle on the most prosperous plots of land.

RELOCATION OF THE JEWS

Hitler's quest for lebensraum did not stop in Poland. As the Nazis marched across eastern Europe, the Germans controlled and contained the Jews by moving them into small sections of towns and cities, called ghettos. The Jews were forced to leave all their belongings behind and could only bring necessities, such as one change of clothing and bedding. They also were given insufficient rations of food.

Above: *Life in the Kovno ghetto in Lithuania.*

Below: *A 1936 illustration entitled "All is well at school now the Jews have gone." Hitler is shown leading Jewish children away from school while Aryan Germans cheer.*

TIME LINE
1938–1939

November 9–10, 1938
Kristallnacht—Night of Broken Glass. Jewish businesses are destroyed and 30,000 Jews are taken to concentration camps.

September 1, 1939
Nazis invade Poland. Jews in Germany are forbidden to be outdoors after 8 P.M. in winter and 9 P.M. in summer.

MEASURES AGAINST JEWS TONIGHT

"a) Only such measures may be taken which do not jeopardize German life or property.
b) Business establishments and homes of Jews may be destroyed but not looted.
c) In business streets special care is to be taken that non-Jewish establishments will be safeguarded.

After arrests have been carried out the appropriate concentration camp is to be contacted with a view to a quick transfer."

Message from SS-Gruppenführer Heydrich to all state police main offices and field offices.

Above: *Life in the ghettos was one of extreme poverty. This photograph taken in 1941 shows three destitute young children on the pavement in the Warsaw ghetto.*

"Buses arrive in Hadamar several times a week with a large number of these victims. School children in the neighborhood know these vehicles and say: 'Here comes the murder wagon.' ... Old people are saying 'on no account will I go into a state hospital!' After the feeble-minded, the old will be next in line as useless mouths to feed."

Letter to Reich minister of justice from Roman Catholic Bishop of Limburg, August 13, 1941, expressing local populace's concern over systematic killing of disabled people. Despite letters like these, Pope John Paul II spoke later of the shame he felt that the Catholic Church kept silent about Nazi atrocities carried out during the war. ✉

TIME TO WAIT

These ghettos actually served as holding areas until the people could be transported to concentration camps and, later, death camps. Many people died of starvation, disease, and exposure to cold. The period of time in the ghetto was one of waiting and uncertainty. Some attempted to keep life as normal as possible, secretly holding classes for children and conducting religious ceremonies. Others, such as those living in the Kovno ghetto in Lithuania, looked at this time as one of preparation for the future. During their three years in the Kovno ghetto, people collected and hid everything from Nazi directives to sketches and diary entries. They wanted a physical record of Nazi atrocities. After the war, those who survived returned to exhume the historical remains.

DEADLY INTENTIONS

In 1939, Hitler authorized a program of extermination called T-4. This "euthanasia" program was marketed to the public as a solution for those living a "Life without Hope." Mentally and physically disabled people were sterilized, starved, and killed by lethal injection as early as 1939. In 1940, the first gassings began at an asylum at Grafeneck, Germany. Growing awareness and public outcry from churches brought attention to the T-4 program. In August of 1941, Hitler gave the "order" to stop all euthanasia programs, but that was only a ploy to stop the protests. About 275,000 disabled people were murdered under this program.

EINSATZGRUPPEN

When the mass murder of Jews began, the crimes were committed by mobile killing squads called

Above: *Jewish women are forced to rebuild a ghetto wall in Kovno after a bombing raid in 1941.*

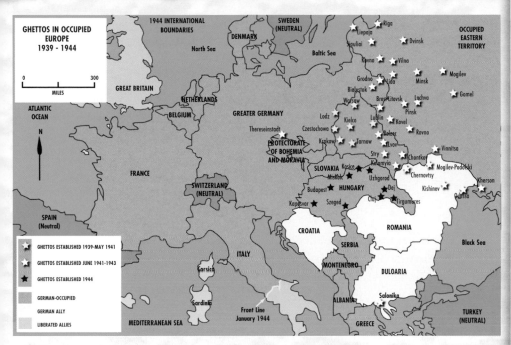

GHETTOS IN OCCUPIED EUROPE 1939 - 1944

Above: A map showing the main ghettos in Europe between 1939 and 1944.

Einsatzgruppen. These units of between four hundred and five hundred men followed the Wehrmacht—the German army as it invaded the Soviet Union in 1941. Their job was to travel from shtetl to shtetl, collecting valuables and then murdering the Jewish residents. Sometimes the victims were forced to dig a mass grave before they were shot; other times the bodies were burned on large fire pits. In the town of Ejszyszki, Lithuania, four thousand Jews were murdered in two days. In 1942, Heinrich Himmler called a halt to this practice because it caused too much

"We could each pull four or five of the smaller ones [tomatoes] from the vines and place them next to each other onto a piece of torn-off cloth rag. A couple of safety pins secured the ends of the rag inside our pants.... Naturally this required some very gingerly walking! Each successful delivery ... was a moment of triumph for us."

From *An Unbroken Chain*, written by Holocaust survivor Henry Oertelt.

TIME LINE 1939–1940

September 3, 1939
England and France declare war on Germany.

September 27, 1939
Warsaw surrenders. Nazis and Soviets divide up Poland.

October 1939
Nazis begin "euthanasia" program in Germany.

November 23, 1939
Yellow stars required to be worn by Polish Jews over age ten.

February 12, 1940
First deportation of German Jews into occupied Poland.

April 9, 1940
Nazis invade Denmark and Norway.

Left: *An Einsatzgruppen soldier, part of a mobile killing unit, shoots a Jewish prisoner in Russia, 1941.*

"Above all, we have been put under an obligation to remember, to record events and facts, to describe people and characters, images and important moments; to record in writing, drawing, in painting—in any way available to us."

Diary entry from Jewish lawyer Avraham Tory, who was held at the Kovno ghetto.

Above: *The Dutch Jew Anne Frank wrote the most famous diary of the Holocaust while in hiding in Holland.*

Above: *An example of one type of currency issued for use by residents of the Jewish ghettos.*

Above: *Two little boys from the Kovno ghetto shown wearing the Star of David.*

Left: *A sword that once belonged to an SS commander.*

emotional stress on the shooters. By the time this practice was stopped, the Einsatzgruppen had killed about 1.5 million Jews.

RESCUE AND RESISTANCE

Resistance to the Nazis was both difficult and dangerous. In Dolhyhnov, Lithuania, the entire ghetto was murdered when two boys escaped. Despite this, faced with annihilation, millions of persecuted Jews in Nazi Germany and the occupied countries found ways to resist persecution. Thousands of Jews fled to join the Allied fight against the Nazis, while others formed their own units to wage guerrilla warfare. In eastern Europe, thousands of Jews banded together in family camps or groups and hid in the forests where they defended themselves with weapons in the face of enemy persecution.

THE WARSAW GHETTO UPRISING

Between 1942 and 1943, underground resistance units had developed in about one-fourth of the ghettos. Because weapons had been confiscated from Jews long before World War II broke out, weapons had to first be smuggled into the ghettos. The Warsaw Ghetto Uprising, led by Mordecai Anielewicz and the Jewish Combat Organization of Warsaw, was the largest and most symbolic armed revolt against the Nazis. On April 19, 1943, in an attempt to halt deportations from the ghetto, a group of armed men and women attacked the Nazis with handguns, gasoline grenades, and one machine gun. Armed fighting engulfed the streets of the ghetto. The Nazis finally ended the resistance on May 16, although sporadic fighting continued.

> "I was 16 at the time and had been in the conspiracy, so to say, for some time. The Germans having closed all the high schools, I participated in classes that met secretly in private homes in groups numbering less than twelve. The beginning of the Uprising was greeted with much euphoria. At last we would no longer allow ourselves to be slaughtered like sheep. It was high time to say enough."
>
> **The Recollections of Witold Górski, who fought in the Warsaw Ghetto Uprising.**

CAMP RESISTANCE

Although resistance in the camps meant almost immediate death for prisoners, prisoners still made attempts. At Auschwitz, prisoners used gun powder, smuggled in from a munitions factory, to blow up Crematorium IV. At the Sobibór extermination camp, eleven SS guards were killed when prisoners revolted. Three hundred escaped, but a third of them were recaptured and executed.

AID FROM OTHERS

Rescue of Jews, although not common, took many forms. Children were hidden in convents, sent to other countries, and hidden in attics and basements. One of the most famous Holocaust victims was a young German girl named Anne Frank. Having fled to Amsterdam, Anne and her family were hidden in an attic apartment behind an office. With the help of Miep Gies, the family hid for two years until the Nazis were tipped off and they were sent to Auschwitz. Anne was then sent to the Bergen-Belsen camp where she died of typhoid fever.

Above: Frightened Jewish residents are taken from the Warsaw ghetto by soldiers after the Jewish uprising.

November 15, 1941
Reichskommissar for Ostland
To: Reich Minister for the Occupied Eastern Territories
RE: Execution of Jews

Will you please inform me whether your inquiry of 31st October should be interpreted as a directive to liquidate all the Jews in Ostland? Is this to be done regardless of age, sex, and economic requirements (for instance, the Wehrmacht's demand for skilled workers in the armament industry)? Of course the cleansing of Ostland of Jews is a most important task; its solution, however, must be in accord with the requirements of war production. . .

Loshe
Reichskommissar for Ostland

A **letter** from a Nazi commander in Ostland seeking clarification as to which Jews should be murdered.

TIME LINE
1940

May 1940
Nazis invade France, Belgium, Holland (the Netherlands), and Luxembourg.

June 1940
Nazis occupy Paris, France.

November 1940
Hungary, Romania, and Slovakia become Nazi allies.

November 15, 1940
The Warsaw ghetto is sealed off.

Below: Concentration camp prisoners were made to wear wool uniforms like this one.

"One day, the brothers asked Mrs. Nielsen to help them find a fisherman who would take them to Sweden, where they could escape the Nazis. . . . As soon as she heard the story, she offered to hide the boys in her home while she arranged for a boat which would take them to Sweden. . . . Through the fishermen, the Danish underground learned of Mrs. Nielsen's act and contacted her . . . (as she) was ideally placed to act as liaison between them and the underground. She accepted, and over a hundred refugees passed through her home on the way to Sweden during the following weeks."

An account of Swede Ellen Nielsen's efforts to shelter Jewish children during the war, extracted from *Women in the Resistance and in the Holocaust*, edited by Vera Laska and published in 1983.

Above: *The railroad track at what used to be the Treblinka concentration camp.*

In January 1942, Reinhard Heydrich, an SS leader, gathered together a team of high-ranking Nazis to discuss what should be done about the "Jewish problem." The result of this gathering, called the Wannsee Conference, was the "Final Solution." The Nazis would use the newest technology in poisonous gassing to exterminate all of the Jews, Gypsies, and prisoners of war in Europe. The Nazis wasted no time transforming work camps into extermination camps and creating new camps for exterminations only. The main camps were Treblinka, Belzec, Sobibór, and Chelmno, all in Poland.

"[A]nd we say that the war will not end as the Jews imagine it will, ... but the result of this war will be the complete annihilation of the Jews.

"And the further this war spreads, the further will spread this fight against the world of the [Jew], and they will be used as food for every prison camp ... the hour will come when the enemy of all times, or at least of the last thousand years, will have played his part to the end."

Adolph Hitler speaking to a crowd at the Sports Palace in Berlin, January 30, 1942.

LIQUIDATION OF THE GHETTOS

As soon as the "Final Solution" was put into motion, the Nazis began liquidating ghettos all over Europe. Jews who had been confined to ghettos were rounded up and loaded onto railroad cars. The ghetto was then destroyed, often by setting it ablaze, to ensure that no Jews were hiding there. Two hundred people were jammed into each cattle car. Forced to stand, often for days, they traveled without food, water, or bathroom facilities. In the summer, people died from heat exhaustion, and in the winter, many froze to death. The weak often did not survive the trip to the camps.

CAMP SELECTION

At many camps, upon arrival, men and women were separated into two lines. Most young children and elderly people were sent immediately to the gas chamber. Women who refused to give up their babies or were pregnant also were sent to the gas chamber. The gas chambers were disguised as shower rooms, so that prisoners would not panic and would proceed in an orderly fashion into the chamber. At Auschwitz, Poland, prisoners were told to place any valuables in piles and to carefully fold their clothing or hang it on a hook since they would be returning after taking a shower. Once in the "shower room," which could hold as many as two thousand people in some camps, the doors were closed and the Zyklon-B pellets were dropped into the chamber through a shoot from the roof. The pellets create a poisonous gas when exposed to air. It took ten to twenty minutes for all of the people in the chamber to die from the poison. The bodies were then removed and burned in crematorium ovens or on large open-air fire pits. In Auschwitz

Left: *Jewish women and children from Hungary await the selection process after getting off the train at Auschwitz-Birkenau.*

Above: *Prisoners were forced to sleep as many as three or four to a wooden bunk, stacked four levels high.*

alone, approximately one million people died in the gas chambers.

SURVIVING SELECTION

Those who were deemed strong enough to work were not immediately sent to the chambers. Instead, they were herded into another building where they were stripped of their identities; their heads were shaved,

Above: *Birkenau main gate and guard tower, viewed from inside the camp. The rail line leading into the camp, and all inmates, passed under the archway.*

Left: *This photograph shows Jews from Carpatho-Ruthenia at Auschwitz in June 1944. They are "passed" as fit for work after a delousing and head-shaving, part of the registration process at the camp. The photograph was taken by SS guards for reasons that are still not known.*

TIME LINE
1941

March 1, 1941
Himmler orders a second camp to be built at Auschwitz.

April 6, 1941
Nazis invade Yugoslavia.

June 22, 1941
Nazis invade the Soviet Union

July 31, 1941
Göring instructs Heydrich to prepare for "Final Solution."

September 1, 1941
German Jews ordered to wear yellow stars.

"Our poorly lit train station . . . was brightly lit and bustling with noise and commotion. . . . Everyone knew what this meant. They had come to liquidate our ghetto. The Market Square 'selections' came first. They forced every man, woman, and child to walk in front of a Gestapo officer. After a quick inspection, he would decide who went to the right, who went to the left. They would keep a small group of young, strong men and women for slave labor. The armed Nazis, their helpers, and the frightening dogs would lead the rest of the people to the railroad station. They would pack them into the waiting cattle cars and send them off to the gas chambers of Treblinka."

Sabina Zimering, from her book *Hiding in the Open*.

> "I remember a very sad day, when six of my friends were hanged by the SS. During all my time in the camps, I have seen maybe ten executions by hanging. But these six friends. . . .We shared everything we could find in the kommando. It was very difficult to enter in the camp with food because, each time, we were searched by the guards. And if they found something on you, you were immediately hanged. One day, one of these friends had been searched and the SS found a piece of bread in his pocket. The SS said he had stolen it but, in fact, he had received it from a French worker. The next day, the SS hanged my friend; a public hanging. It was horrible for me."
>
> **Richard Sufit, interned in Drancy (France), then taken to Auschwitz-Birkenau on June 30, 1944.**

and they were forced to wear ill-fitting uniforms. Their names were also stripped from them. They were identified instead by numbers either sewn on their uniforms or tattooed on one of their forearms. Prisoners lived in barracks with hundreds of others and were sent to perform slave labor in quarries or for factories and businesses that helped the Nazi war effort. Most prisoner barracks had no toilets, only a row of buckets with no privacy. Prisoners slept on bunks made of wooden planks, often sleeping five or six to a bunk. Food was scarce and insufficient. Most meals consisted of a small piece of bread, watery soup made with a piece of rotten vegetable, and weak coffee. Because people were so dehydrated and malnourished, they often became ill and died of disease. One of the most dreaded events was roll call. Those prisoners who collapsed were shot on the spot or sent to the gas chambers.

Above: *Many prisoners worked in quarries. Guards were known to push workers off the quarry walls to their death for pure entertainment. This image shows workers at Auschwitz.*

SONDERKOMMANDO

The Nazis committed many atrocious acts, but one of the most sadistic punishments for prisoners was to be assigned to the *Sonderkommando*, the groups of Jewish prisoners forced to perform the "dirty work" for the Nazis. One group was responsible for meeting the trains and deceiving the new arrivals into believing that they were being deloused and disinfected when they were actually going to their death. Sometimes members of the Sonderkommando knew the people going to the gas chambers. Other teams processed the corpses after the gas chambers. Gold teeth were extracted, clothing and valuables were removed, and bodies were cremated. The warehouse in which

Left: *If a prisoner escaped, other prisoners were held responsible and hanged or shot. These prisoners at Auschwitz are being tortured by guards in 1944.*

valuables were stored was called "Kanada" because the Germans thought Canada was a country of great, undiscovered treasure. Although members of the Sonderkommando had better living conditions—decent food and normal clothing—their life expectancy was only several months. The Nazis did not want any witnesses, so every few months all of the Sonderkommandos were gassed. Other prisoners regarded the Sonderkommando with contempt. Author Primo Levi described them as being "akin to collaborators." For this reason, some entered the gas chambers of their own free will rather than having to perform the grizzly tasks assigned. The Sonderkommando at Birkenau, Poland, organized an uprising that took place on October 7, 1944. Aided by women from the nearby

Above: *Gold teeth extracted from corpses at Auschwitz.*

Monowitz camp, who worked in a munitions factory, gunpowder was smuggled to the Sonderkommando at Birkenau. One gas chamber was destroyed, but all of the participants of the uprising died in the explosion and its aftermath.

MEDICAL EXPERIMENTS

Two hundred Nazi doctors stationed at various camps made selections and performed medical experiments on

Below: *This photograph was taken in 1944 by a camp inmate at Birkenau assigned to one of the special prisoner teams (Sonderkommando) who were forced to work in the gas chamber/crematoria. This photo shows prisoners burning corpses freshly removed from the gassing facility at Crematorium-V.*

TIME LINE
1941–1943

September 17, 1941
Beginning of general deportation of German Jews.

December 7, 1941
Japanese attack Pearl Harbor. The following day the United States and Great Britain declare war on Japan.

January 20, 1942
Wannsee Conference to coordinate the "Final Solution."

February 2, 1943
Germans surrender at Stalingrad.

"They were taken by groups into a big room which looked exactly like a shower room, but when the room was filled with prisoners, the doors were closed and the gas Cyclon B was released through holes in the floor and ceiling. In about ten minutes all who were in the room would be dead. A special kommando called the Sonderkommando, consisting of about eight hundred strong young Jewish prisoners selected from the Jewish transports, transferred the corpses from the gas chambers to the crematoria."

Petro Mirchuk, a Ukranian Jew, testifies as to what happened at Auschwitz.

> "He grabbed her by the neck and proceeded to beat her head to a bloody pulp. He hit her, slapped her, boxed her, always her head—screaming at the top of his voice, 'You want to escape, don't you. You can't escape now. You are going to burn like the others, you are going to croak, you dirty Jew.' As I watched, I saw her two beautiful, intelligent eyes disappear under a layer of blood. And in a few seconds, her straight, pointed nose was a flat, broken, bleeding mass. Half an hour later, Dr. Mengele returned to the hospital. He took a piece of perfumed soap out of his bag and, whistling gaily with a smile of deep satisfaction on his face, he began to wash his hands."

Dr. Gisella Perl, inmate at Auschwitz.

Below: *Josef Mengele, the "Angel of Death."*

selected victims. Medical experiments fell into three categories: those designed to aid the Reich personnel in developing combat gear, those designed to aid pharmaceutical companies with research on drugs and treatment of disease, and those designed to help the Nazis develop a "pure" Aryan race. What all experiments had in common was that they defied any moral and ethical responsibility on the part of the physician. Survival and rescue experiments, for example, were designed to discover how much the human body could endure when placed under harsh or stressed conditions. The most infamous Nazi doctor was Dr. Josef Mengele, known as the "Angel of Death." Mengele performed his racial experiments at Auschwitz from 1943 to 1945, mostly on sets of twins and dwarfs. "Mengele's children," as the twins were called, initially received special treatment, but they later were subjected to a much crueler fate.

As part of his racial hygiene theory, children were injected with dye in an attempt to change their eye color. This often resulted in blindness and death. Twins were given blood transfusions of the wrong blood type, which produced massive headaches, high fever, and

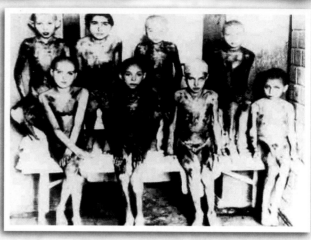

Above: *Both Jewish and Gypsy children were the victims of Josef Mengele, the "Angel of Death." Twins especially were subjected to painful, grotesque experiments. This photograph shows children who survived at Auschwitz.*

often death. Other children were subjected to castration, amputation, and other frightening and painful surgical procedures, always performed without an anesthetic.

POLISH EXTERMINATION CAMPS

Extermination camps, or killing centers, were designed for instant and secret death. The first extermination camp, Chelmno, was built 45 miles (72 km) from Lodz in western Poland and opened in December 1941. With the verbal directive of the "Final Solution" in 1942, Hitler and Himmler set about enacting Operation Reinhard—a scheme to exterminate the Jewish population of Warsaw, Krakow, Lublin, Radom, and Lvov. According to the Nazis, these areas were inhabited by over two million Jews. The actual killing was to be carried out in three death camps—Belzec, Sobibór, and Treblinka. These three camps were

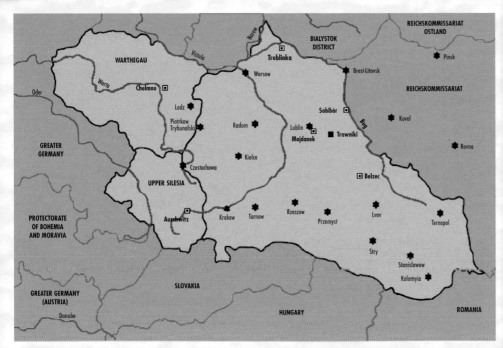

Above: *Map showing the location of the main extermination camps built as part of the "Final Solution."*

TIME LINE
1943–1944

March 1, 1943
In New York, American Jews hold a mass rally.

May 19, 1943
Nazis declare Berlin to be *Judenfrei* ("cleansed of Jews").

July 9–10, 1943
Allies (including the United States and Great Britain) land in Sicily.

March 24, 1944
U.S. president Roosevelt issues a statement condemning German and Japanese ongoing "crimes against humanity."

June 6, 1944
D-Day: Allied landings in Normandy.

June–July, 1944
The New York Times reports via the *London Daily Telegraph* that over one million Jews have already been killed by Nazis.

built in secluded areas and used carbon monoxide gas chambers to kill Jews. Under Operation Reinhard, an estimated 1.7 million Jews and 52,000 Gypsies were murdered. There were only 120 known survivors.

OTHER KILLING CENTERS

Majdanek outside Lublin, Poland, was initially built for Poles, Polish Jews, and Polish resisters and was primarily a forced work camp. Due to resistance uprisings in the Treblinka and Sobibór camps, in 1943 the SS in Berlin decided to kill the remaining Jews in Majdanek. In an action code-named Operation *Erntefest* ("Harvest Festival"), eighteen thousand Jews were shot while music was played to drown out the sound of gunfire. Auschwitz, located in Poland, was the largest of the German camps and was

Above: *Crematorium ovens were used to dispose of dead bodies. Ashes were then placed in urns and buried. Some ash was sold to grieving survivors, who thought that these were the remains of relatives.*

"Werner Rhode hated his work, and Hans Konig was deeply disgusted by the job.... [they] had to get drunk before they appeared on the ramp. Only two doctors performed the selections without any stimulants of any kind: Dr. Josef Mengele and Dr. Fritz Klein. Dr. Mengele was particularly cold and cynical. He [Mengele] once told me that there are only two gifted people in the world, Germans and Jews, and it's a question of who will be superior. So he decided that they had to be destroyed."

Dr. Ella Lingens, an Austrian doctor who was imprisoned at Auschwitz for attempting to hide some Jewish friends, describes how Mengele relished his role as selector.

Left: *SS soldiers bury the dead at the Belsen, Germany, concentration camp after the liberation of the camp by the Allies. In the six weeks after the British arrived a further thirteen thousand camp victims died.*

a complex containing a labor camp, a concentration camp, and an extermination camp. Auschwitz I, a concentration camp, was used mainly as a prison for political criminals, but it also had a gas chamber and crematorium. Auschwitz II, or Auschwitz-Birkenau, had the largest number of prisoners and was constructed when the Nazis realized Auschwitz I was not large enough.

Four large crematoriums that included disrobing areas, gas chambers, and ovens were built in Auschwitz-Birkenau. Zyklon-B, a rat poison, was first used there. Auschwitz III, called Monowitz, was built for slave laborers so they could work at the Buna synthetic rubber works. A series of sub-camps for slave labor were also attached to Auschwitz III. Workers regularly were subjected to the selection process where the sick were sent to the gas chambers at Birkenau.

"By way of the redistribution camp Westerbork, I ended up in Auschwitz. . . . Of the 1,200 people in our transport, 1,000 were gassed to death immediately; 120 men and 60-80 women were allowed to stay alive a little longer. At the time, the average time of survival was three months. . . Everything was taken away from us, except for a pair of glasses and a belt. Within a few hours, we had been reduced to bald-shaven, rag-clad souls identified by number, who from that day on vegetated in a state of complete abandonment, hopelessness, and wretchedness. Our bleak life was full of suffering, disease, hunger, and cold and was constantly threatened by the gas chamber."

Max Hamburger, a Dutch Jew, writes about his experience at Auschwitz.

Above: *When Allied troops first discovered camps, they had no idea the extent of what they were seeing. Prisoners at this camp at Buchenwald were so thin from malnutrition that they appeared to be walking corpses.*

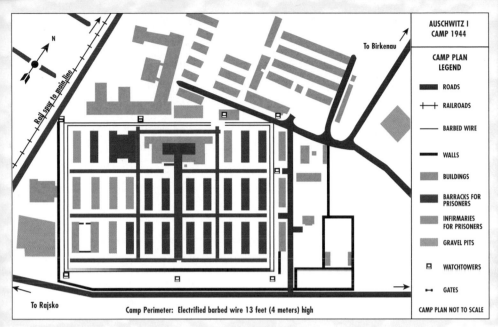

Above: *Plan of the camp at Auschwitz 1.*

AUSCHWITZ I
CAMP 1944

To Birkenau

CAMP PLAN LEGEND

▬▬▬	ROADS
┼┼┼	RAILROADS
────	BARBED WIRE
▬▬▬	WALLS
▬	BUILDINGS
▬	BARRACKS FOR PRISONERS
▬	INFIRMARIES FOR PRISONERS
▬	GRAVEL PITS
⊟	WATCHTOWERS
⊢⊣	GATES

CAMP PLAN NOT TO SCALE

N

Rail spur to main line

To Rajsko

Camp Perimeter: Electrified barbed wire 13 feet (4 meters) high

TIME LINE
1944

August 4, 1944
Anne Frank and family arrested by Gestapo in Amsterdam.

August 6, 1944
Lodz, the last Jewish ghetto in Poland, is liquidated.

November 25, 1944
Himmler orders the destruction of crematories at Auschwitz.

LIBERATION

On July 23, 1944, the first Soviet troops stumbled upon Majdanek in Poland. On January 27, 1945, Auschwitz-Birkenau was liberated. The soldiers found hundreds of sick, starving people, half of whom died shortly after the Allies arrived. The Nazis were forced to leave so quickly that they left rooms filled with piles of eyeglasses, shoes, gold from human teeth, and many written records of the atrocities that had taken place. Although they attempted to blow up the crematorium, the starving people and piles of dead bodies were still there to tell the story. The liberators' first response was to give the people food. Unfortunately, many died soon after liberation because they ate foods that were too rich for their weakened systems.

Above: *This photo was taken at the Buchenwald concentration camp just weeks after the liberation. Soldiers laid wreaths over piles of dead bodies during visits to the camp.*

Above: *Eyeglasses were taken from prisoners upon arrival because the Nazis planned to sell them.*

"In April 1945, I was freed, more dead than alive, from the Buchenwald Concentration Camp by the 8th American Army under the leadership of General Patton. I was so weak at the time that I could no longer walk. I remember one particular night: I was lying in bed, consumed with fever. The good American food didn't agree with my drained stomach and my weakened bowels, and only increased my exhaustion. I got the feeling that 'if I fall asleep now, I won't wake up tomorrow!' At that moment, I decided that I couldn't allow myself to die. If I did, I wouldn't be able to fulfill my assignment: to bear witness to that which had happened to us."

Max Hamburger, Dutch Jew.

Above: *Poster advertising the film* Der Ewige Jude *(The Eternal Jew), shown in 1933. The Nazis used propaganda to portray Jews as "vermin" infiltrating the "sanctity" of Aryan life.*

> "Propaganda has only one object—to conquer the masses. Every means that furthers this aim is good; every means that hinders it is bad."
>
> **Joseph Goebbels' diaries.**

The mere mention of the Holocaust today usually evokes feelings of sorrow for the lives lost, anger at the perpetrators, and guilt for not having done enough to stop Hitler and the Nazis. At the time, people in the countries fighting the Nazis knew Jews were being persecuted, and many undoubtedly knew what was going on in the camps, but anti-Semitic feelings prevailing in Europe and the United States created pressure to not become involved. People did not want to hear about the plight of the Jews. Some, however, refused to be silent about Nazi atrocities and continue to speak out today.

PROPAGANDA

One of the Nazis most effective methods for brainwashing people was the use of propaganda. Hitler himself declared in *Mein Kampf* that propaganda was one of the most effective ways of getting a message across to the German public. Once Hitler was in power, he set up the *Reichministerium für Volksaufklärung und Propaganda* (Ministry for Popular Enlightenment and Propaganda or RMVP) under Dr. Joseph Goebbels. In German newspapers, anti–

Below: *Propaganda poster showing Hitler as the knight in shining armor leading the Germans into battle and out of despair.*

Right: *Dr. Seuss created the Sneetches to draw attention to discrimination such as anti-Semitism.*

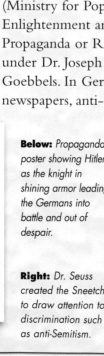
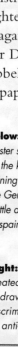

Semitic cartoons portrayed Jews as the devil, child killers, and molesters of women. In children's books, the young were warned about taking candy from Jews because it might be poisoned. Before movies were shown in theaters, anti-Semitic short films, such as *Der Ewige Jude* (The Eternal Jew), depicted Jews as sub-human rats that infested a host country. Hitler, on the other hand, was likened to a Godlike savior.

CARTOONS

Some, however, did make a mockery of the "silly little man with the moustache." Arthur Szyk, a native Pole living in the United States, unleashed his paintbrush against the atrocities of the Nazis and became America's leading political caricaturist during World War II. Arthur Szyk's "A Madman's Dream" depicts Hitler seated on a throne with the world in his lap and a "Jew-skin" rug underneath him. Uncle Sam and John Bull are in chains pleading with him. Dr. Seuss, known for his tongue-twisting children's books, started his career as a political cartoonist for several different magazines. Theodor ("Ted") Seuss Geisel was born on March 2, 1904, in Springfield, Massachusetts. During World War II, Seuss drew editorial cartoons for the left-wing New York newspaper *PM*. The story "The Sneetches" was inspired by Seuss's opposition to anti-Semitism and other forms of discrimination. In the story, some Sneetches have a green star on their belly, and the

"I had one purpose: I wanted to, wherever I could at this particular time, point out as strongly as I could that the United States was going to get involved in this war."

Interview with "Dr. Seuss," 1976.

presence or absence of these stars is the basis for discrimination. At the end of the story, the Sneetches learn that neither plain-bellied nor star-bellied sneetches are superior, and they are able to get along and become friends. The story teaches that all people are the same on the inside, despite outward differences.

TIME LINE
1945

January 6, 1945
Soviets liberate Budapest, freeing over 80,000 Jews.

January 17, 1945
Liberation of Warsaw by the Soviets.

January 27, 1945
Soviet troops liberate Auschwitz. By this time, an estimated 1.5 million Jews have been murdered there.

Below: *Arthur Szyk's "A Madman's Dream" ridicules Hitler. It depicts him seated on a throne with the world in his lap and a "Jew-skin" rug underneath him. Uncle Sam and John Bull are in chains pleading with him.*

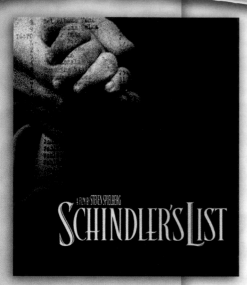

Above: A poster from Spielberg's Schindler's List (1993).

Above: Set during the Warsaw Ghetto Uprising, The Pianist (2002), directed by Roman Polanski, illustrates what life was like for those forced to live in hiding.

THE HOLOCAUST ON FILM

The suffering of the Jewish people in Germany was portrayed on film as early as 1940. At that time, major American film studios refused to portray Hitler in a negative light, but Charlie Chaplin produced his own film, *The Great Dictator* (1940), in which he criticized Hitler. In Chaplin's movie, a poor Jewish barber is persecuted under an anti-Semitic dictatorship. The barber, however, looks similar to Adenoid Hynkel, the fictional dictator, and is one day mistaken for the dictator. Despite its serious subject, the film, like much of Chaplin's work, is humorous. Chaplin later claimed that he never would have made light of the Holocaust had he known the extent of the violence. In 1964, Sidney Lumet's *The Pawnbroker* portrayed a Holocaust survivor experiencing flashbacks of his time spent in a Nazi camp. Not until 1978, however, did movies come close to accurately portraying Nazi atrocities. *The Holocaust,* a nine-hour mini-series shown on American television, prompted discussions about Holocaust history in both the United States and Europe. More recently, Steven Spielberg's *Schindler's List* (1993) has received critical acclaim for the accurate depiction of historical events combined with the absence of violent scenes. Filmed in black and white, Spielberg's academy award-winning movie exposed the history of the Holocaust to more people than any other film in the twentieth century.

HOLOCAUST IN LITERATURE

Several writers have dealt with the Holocaust and its aftermath. In 1958, Nobel Peace Prize winner Elie Wiesel wrote the book *Night* based on his own experiences in Birkenau, Auschwitz, and Buchenwald. Since its publication, many other survivors have summoned the courage to relive the past and write

"Today is history. Today will be remembered. Years from now the young will ask with wonder about this day. Today is history and you are part of it. Six hundred years ago when elsewhere they were footing the blame for the Black Death, Casimir the Great—so called—told the Jews they could come to Krakow. They came. They trundled their belongings into the city. They settled. They took hold. They prospered in business, science, education, the arts. With nothing they came and with nothing they flourished. For six centuries there has been a Jewish Krakow. By this evening, those six centuries will be a rumor. They never happened."

Quote from SS officer Amon Goeth in Steven Spielberg's *Schindler's List* (1993).

their own autobiographies. In Simon Wiesenthal's *The Sunflower*, a dying Nazi soldier asks for forgiveness from a Jewish prisoner. The author raises the question "What would you do if you were the prisoner?" and includes responses from prominent twentieth-century personalities such as the Dalai Lama and Dith Pran, a survivor of the Cambodian killing fields. Another book, *I Never Saw Another Butterfly*, immortalizes a collection of artwork and poetry created by the children of the Theresienstadt, Czechoslovakia, ghetto.

Above: *Holocaust survivor Elie Wiesel is a Nobel Peace Prize winner and champion for human rights.*

"First they came for the Jews and I did not speak out—because I was not a Jew.

Then they came for the communists and I did not speak out—because I was not a communist.

Then they came for the trade unionists and I did not speak out—because I was not a trade unionist.

Then they came for me—and there was no one left to speak out for me."

A poem by Pastor Martin Niemoller, Berlin, 1939. Niemoller was a pastor in the German Confessing Church and spent over eight years in a Nazi concentration camp.

Left: *Charlie Chaplin starred in several films that poked fun at dictators such as Hitler. Chaplin was hated by the German leader.*

TIME LINE
1945–1947

April 23, 1945
Soviet troops reach Berlin.

April 29, 1945
U.S. Seventh Army liberates Dachau.

April 30, 1945
Hitler commits suicide in his bunker.

May 7, 1945
Unconditional German surrender signed by General Gustav Jodl, chief of staff of the German army.

October 1946
Nuremberg court issues its first verdicts.

1947
Britain renounces mandate in Palestine, paving the way for the creation of the Jewish country of Israel.

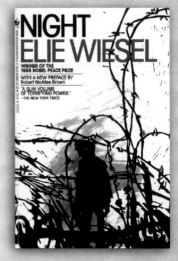

NIGHT ELIE WIESEL
WINNER OF THE 1986 NOBEL PEACE PRIZE
WITH A NEW PREFACE BY Robert McAfee Brown
"A SLIM VOLUME OF TERRIFYING POWER." —THE NEW YORK TIMES

Above: *After a ten-year silence, Elie Wiesel wrote the book Night. This book captured the attention of readers everywhere and brought worldwide attention to the Holocaust.*

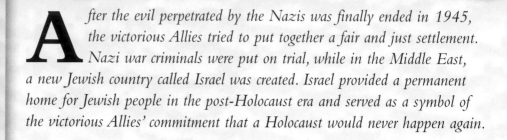

After the evil perpetrated by the Nazis was finally ended in 1945, the victorious Allies tried to put together a fair and just settlement. Nazi war criminals were put on trial, while in the Middle East, a new Jewish country called Israel was created. Israel provided a permanent home for Jewish people in the post-Holocaust era and served as a symbol of the victorious Allies' commitment that a Holocaust would never happen again.

> "The Nazi Holocaust, which engulfed millions of Jews in Europe, proved anew the urgency of the reestablishment of the Jewish State, which would solve the problem of Jewish homelessness by opening the gates to all Jews and lifting the Jewish people to equality in the family of nations. . . . This recognition by the United Nations of the right of the Jewish people to establish their independent State may not be revoked. It is, moreover, the self-evident right of the Jewish people to be a nation, as all other nations, in its own sovereign State."

David Ben-Gurion, the chairman of the Jewish Agency for Palestine, on May 14, 1948.

Below: *This photograph was used after the war by a Jewish father in France, in an attempt to locate his four-year old son, Albeit Smiel Vieder. It is likely that many copies of this photo were circulated in France.*

RETURN TO LIFE

After the jubilation and realization that they were free, Holocaust survivors faced the task of returning to real life. Some returned home to find their home occupied by another family or destroyed by bombs. Displaced persons camps were set up to help survivors reunite with family and friends and readjust to society. There, many people waited to be admitted to countries like the United States and to Palestine. To help World War II survivors, the United States established the Displaced Persons Act of 1948. This act allowed for fewer restrictions on immigration to the United States, but it also contained strong anti-Semitic sentiments and restricted the number of Jews allowed to immigrate. The British, under pressure from Arabs in the region, also strictly controlled the number of Jews entering Palestine.

A NEW STATE IS BORN

The United Nations, however, recognized the plight of Jews in the aftermath of the Holocaust in Europe, and in 1947, the United Nations Special Commission on Palestine (UNSCOP) recommended that Palestine be divided into an Arab state and a Jewish state (Israel). The Jews accepted this split, but the Arabs rejected it. The plan was adopted on November 29, 1947, largely due to the support of Harry S. Truman, but it soon became painfully obvious that this plan would not work. The Arabs declared war to rid Palestine of Jews. By the end of 1949, Israel had

> "I got shipped, um, got shipped to France and finally wound up in a, in an orphanage in Fublaines. It, which is just on the outskirts of Paris. And I was one of the youngest children there, and I didn't speak to anybody except Miriam (a friend of Irene's), who was about, I guess about seven years older. She seemed like almost a mother figure in a sense to me, because she would, I had these long curls and she would fuss with them and she just was very compassionate, and I, um, the other children— I was the only child there with a number, so I also felt that there was something wrong with me. I felt that I had done something horrible, that I had gotten the number and nobody else did. Most of these children had escaped somehow by hiding, or their parents had temporarily given them over and some were subsequently reunited with parents, and some just had family members and they were just waiting to be shipped, too, and you know, things like that."

Survivor Irene Hizme describes life in a Catholic orphanage in postwar France.

declared its independence, and cease-fire lines were formally established. The land originally designated as an Arab Palestinian state was now part of either Israel or Jordan, and the holy city of Jerusalem was divided into a western part controlled by Israel and an eastern part controlled by Jordan. In the decades since the founding of Israel, Jews and Arabs have fought over territory, including that which previously belonged to Egypt, Jordan, and Syria. Subsequent treaties and peace negotiations between Israel, its Arab neighbors, and the Palestinians have resulted in redefined borders, but the fundamental conflict between Israel and the Palestinians has yet to be resolved.

A SEARCH FOR JUSTICE

In 1942, long before Adolf Hitler committed suicide in a bunker below Berlin, the Allied powers, declared the Nazis would be prosecuted for the mass murder of Jews. After the Nazi defeat, in October 1945, the Nazi criminal trials began in Nuremberg Germany.

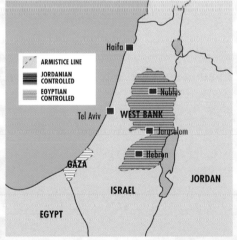

Above: A map showing the creation of the state of Israel as proposed by the UN in 1947.

Legend:
- ARAB STATE
- JEWISH STATE
- JERUSALEM: INTERNATIONAL CITY

Below: A map showing the revised area of Israel after the 1949 conflict.

Legend:
- ARMISTICE LINE
- JORDANIAN CONTROLLED
- EGYPTIAN CONTROLLED

Right: At the Nuremberg Trials, 22 Nazis faced accusations of war crimes, but many more escaped justice.

TIME LINE
1948–1967

1948
UN Resolution 181 formally divides Palestine into two, creating the country of Israel.

1949
Israeli-Arab war ends.

1952
Reparations deal signed between West Germany and Israel.

1956
Israel occupies Gaza Strip.

1967
Six-Day War begins.

"I have never felt able to describe my emotional reaction when I first came face to face with indisputable evidence of Nazi brutality and ruthless disregard of every shred of decency. . . . I visited every nook and cranny of the camp because I felt it my duty to be in a position from then on to testify at first hand about these things in case there ever grew up at home the belief or assumption that the stories of Nazi brutality were just propaganda."

General Dwight D. Eisenhower, Supreme Commander, Allied Forces, Europe.

Right: *Adolf Eichmann shown during his trial for war crimes. He was executed on May 31, 1962.*

"When I was maybe seven, eight years old, we had recently moved to Washington and on a hot day, we decided to go to the beach. And people told us that there was a lovely beach somewhere in Chesapeake Bay, and we drove down there. And I still remember the sign, because as we drove up, we saw the sign, which said, 'No Jews or dogs allowed.'"

Ruth Fein, American Jewish Historical Society.

Above: *After the war, famous artwork and other valuables confiscated by the Nazis were discovered. Here, General Eisenhower examines Jewish property stolen by the Nazis and uncovered in Switzerland.*

Of the twenty-two major Nazi criminals who were tried by the International Military Tribunal, twelve were sentenced to death and seven received prison sentences ranging from ten years to life. Three were acquitted. Subsequent trials involved Gestapo agents, SS men, and industrialists who were accused of implementing the Nuremberg Race Laws, using slave labor for profit, performing medical experimentation, or selling Zyklon-B. The final set of defendants included camp guards, members of the *Einsatzgruppen*, police officers, and doctors who performed medical experiments. Auschwitz had its own tribunal, which sentenced Commandant Rudolf Hoess to death. Many former Nazis, however, did not receive any sentence at all and were allowed to return to Germany.

"There are 350,000 survivors of the Holocaust alive today . . . There are 350,000 experts who just want to be useful with the remainder of their lives. Please listen to the words and the echoes and the ghosts. And please teach this in your schools."

Steven Spielberg, accepting Academy Award for Best Director for *Schindler's List* (1993).

NAZI HUNTING

Some Nazis fled to other countries, particularly those in South America. Adolf Eichmann, a key figure in the implementation of the "Final Solution," was caught in Buenos Aires, Argentina, in May 1960. He was caught by the Israeli Security Service and executed after his trial. His sentence marks the only time a prisoner has been put to death in Israel. Klaus Barbie, "the butcher of Lyon," was caught and tried in 1987. He received a life sentence in prison. The "Angel of Death," Dr. Josef Mengele, managed to hide from Nazi hunters until his death from drowning in 1979. Today, Nazi hunter and Holocaust survivor Simon Wiesenthal continues to operate a Nazi documentation center in Vienna.

THE UNITED STATES REMEMBERS

In 1978, U.S. president Jimmy Carter established the President's Commission on the Holocaust, which established a memorial to Holocaust victims and survivors. In 1993, The United States Holocaust Memorial Museum opened in Washington, D.C. The museum houses several permanent exhibits including "Remember the Children: Daniel's Story" and "The Holocaust." The building also contains a research library, two theaters, a Wall of Remembrance, and The Hall of Remembrance.

YAD VASHEM

Established in Jerusalem in 1953, Yad Vashem is the Jewish people's memorial to those murdered by the Nazis. It contains the world's largest archive of information on the Holocaust—over sixty-three million pages of documents, almost three hundred thousand photographs, and thousands of films and survivor testimony. Yad Vashem also includes several museums, memorials, and the International Institute for Holocaust Studies.

HOLOCAUST DENIAL

Despite the extensive survivor testimony, documentation, and photographs, some people, called Holocaust deniers, claim that the Holocaust never occurred. Deniers do not dispute the fact that the Nazis hated Jews and discriminated against them; what they do not believe happened is the planned, systematic persecution and murder of six million European Jews. Deniers claim that the film footage, architectural ruins, documents, and testimony from survivors and perpetrators are fabricated.

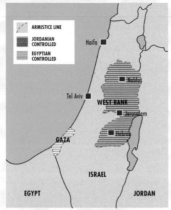

Above: The boundaries of Israel before the 1967 war (top) and after the war (bottom). Subsequent treaties continued to change Israel's borders, but the fundamental conflict between Israelis and Palestinians remains unresolved today.

TIME LINE
1973–2005

1973
Yom Kippur War starts.

1979
Israel and Egypt sign peace treaty.

1982
Israel invades Lebanon.

1987
Mass Palestinian uprising against Israeli occupation of Gaza.

1992
Talks in Oslo, Norway, lead to declaration of principles.

2005
The sixtieth anniversary of the liberation of the extermination and concentration camps.

Left: The United States Holocaust Memorial Museum opened in 1993 and serves as the United States's memorial to the millions of people murdered during the Holocaust.

The Holocaust was perpetrated by a number of individuals who pursued Hitler's goals with great zeal and, in some cases, enjoyment. Many showed no remorse even after the end of the war and testified at the Nuremberg Trials that they believed in what they were doing. On the Jewish side, resistance against this frightening onslaught took many forms. Some people stole food from the Nazis, some kept the Sabbath, and some wrote poetry. Some forms of resistance, however, were more overt, including armed uprisings in the ghettos and Nazi camps.

Adolf Hitler (Nazi) 1889–1945

Adolf Hitler was born on April 20, 1889, in Braunau-am-Inn, Austria. Hitler did not excel at school and left early with the hope of becoming an artist. He fought in a Bavarian regiment during World War I. After the war, he joined the German Workers' Party—later to become the Nazi Party—and quickly gained control. Imprisoned after attempting to overthrow the Weimar Republic government, Hitler emerged even more determined in his quest for power. He became chancellor of Germany in 1933 and abolished democracy soon after. From 1936 onward, he initiated a program of German expansion and a brutal campaign against the Jewish people of Europe. On April 30, 1945, surrounded by Allied troops, Hitler committed suicide with his wife, Eva Braun, whom he had married the day before.

Reinhard Heydrich (Nazi) 1904–1942

Born in Halle, Germany, on March 7, 1904, Reinhard "the Hangman" Heydrich was responsible for organizing the murder of all the Jewish people of Europe. He was described as someone for whom "truth and goodness had no meaning." Heydrich was the leader of the Einsatzgruppen, and he orchestrated the meeting at Wannsee to introduce high-ranking Nazis to the "Final Solution." Heydrich was also responsible for organizing the deportation of European Jews to death camps. In 1942, he died from injures received when a bomb was thrown into his vehicle.

Irma Grese (Nazi) 1923–1945

Born on October 7, 1923, Irma Grese rose to become one of the most notorious female Nazi war criminals. At the age of just nineteen, Irma became a guard at Ravensbruck and was later transferred to the Auschwitz camp. Survivors tell tales of Irma Grese's sadistic treatment of prisoners. She often carried a whip and a pistol, and she seemed to take delight in the selection process. The skins of inmates were found in her quarters, having been made into gruesome lamp shades. Irma Grese was found guilty in the Belsen trial and was hanged for her crimes.

Heinrich Himmler (Nazi) 1900–1945

Heinrich Himmler was born in Munich on October 7, 1900. He studied agriculture but in 1923 joined the Nazi Party as a member of the Sturmabteilung (SA). He went on to be appointed Reichsmarshal of the Schutzstaffel (SS) and became the second most powerful man in Germany. In 1933, Himmler helped set up the first concentration camp in Dachau, Poland. Himmler also created the *Lebensborn* (spring of life) program to care for the children of unwed but "racially pure" mothers, in an effort to increase members of the Aryan race. After the invasion of Poland, this program also included kidnapping Polish children considered to be "racially good." Himmler also came up with the idea of using gas to kill Jews and other prisoners of the Nazis in chambers disguised as shower rooms. Himmler committed suicide in 1945 while awaiting trial for war crimes.

Janusz Korczak (Jewish) 1879–1942

Janusz Korczak was born Henryk Goldsmit in Warsaw, Poland, in 1879. He became a doctor but worked mainly in education and in fighting for children's rights. Under the pseudonym Janusz Korczak, he authored several children's books and books on education. In 1911, he established a Jewish orphanage in Warsaw. After the Germans occupied Warsaw, his orphanage was moved inside the ghetto. When the Warsaw ghetto closed, Korczak and the children of his orphanage were going to be taken to the Treblinka extermination camp. Korczak, a well-known author by this time, refused offers to escape. He traveled with the children in the crowded train to Treblinka and died with them in the gas chambers. Today, many books have been written about him, and many of his own books and poetry have been translated into a host of different languages.

Hannah Senesh (Jewish) 1921–1944

At the age of 22, Hannah Senesh, a native Hungarian, joined the British army and began training to parachute behind German lines and make contact with resistance groups. After spending three months with a resistance group fighting the Nazis in Yugoslavia, she made an unsuccessful attempt to sneak into Hungary. She was captured, and after months of torture, Senesh was placed before a firing squad. She refused to wear a blindfold and stared straight into the eyes of her firing squad. In 1950, Senesh's remains were taken to Israel and re-interred in the military cemetery located on Mount Herz. Senesh started to write a diary at the age of thirteen. Remarkably, she continued to write it until shortly before her death. In 1946, her diary was published in Hebrew.

Mordecai Anielewicz (Jewish) 1920–1943

Mordecai Anielewicz was born to a poor family near Warsaw. After the Nazis declared war on Poland, he attempted to open a route through Romania for Jewish youth fleeing to Israel. He was caught and eventually returned to the Warsaw ghetto, where, in 1940, he began organizing a resistance. On April 19, 1943, Anielewicz and his ghetto fighters, armed only with one machine gun, several hundred pistols, and fifteen rifles, opened fire on German soldiers who were gathering Jews to ship to Treblinka. The Germans took heavy casualties until they set the ghetto's buildings ablaze. Those fleeing the fire were taken to Treblinka. On May 8, the Germans used poison mustard gas to flush out the remaining fighters. About one hundred people escaped through the sewers. Anielewicz was killed by the gas.

Vladka Meed (Jewish) (b. 1923)

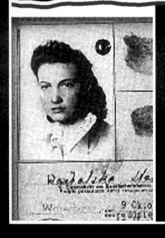

A member of the Jewish Fighting Organization of Warsaw, Vladka Meed lived outside the ghetto among the Poles in order to secure weapons for the resistance. She convinced non-Jews that she was not Jewish, and, using false identification papers, Meed managed to smuggle weapons across the Warsaw ghetto walls. She also smuggled people out of the ghetto and found places for them to hide. Through setting fire to German factories, building homemade grenades, and collecting arms, Meed and her cohorts resisted the Nazis. After the Nazis "liquidated" and closed the ghetto, Meed continued to work for the Polish underground. Meed is now the director of the Holocaust and Jewish Resistance Summer Fellowship Program in Israel.

Simon Wiesenthal (Jewish) (b. 1908)

Simon Wiesenthal was born in Buczacz in the Ukraine. When the Nazis attacked the Soviets, he and his wife were sent to several labor camps. When the "Final Solution" was implemented after 1942, Wiesenthal survived several death camps and a death march to Mauthausen and was liberated just as he was on the brink of death. After the war, Wiesenthal worked tirelessly at gathering information to convict war criminals. After the Nuremberg trials, he became a Nazi hunter and was responsible for bringing many war criminals to justice, including the notorious Adolf Eichmann. Wiesenthal is also an author and the founder of the Simon Wiesenthal Center and the Museum of Tolerance. He lives today in an apartment in Vienna.

Sabina Zimering (Jewish) (b. 1923)

Sabina Zimering, a Polish Jew, was sixteen when World War II broke out. She spent three years hiding from the Nazis after the Gestapo raided her hometown of Piotrkow, Poland, in 1942. False IDs, supplied by Catholic childhood friends, saved her and her sister from the gas chambers of Treblinka. They survived as Catholic Poles in Nazi Germany working at a Gestapo Hotel. After the war, Sabina attended Munich Medical School, received her degree, immigrated to Minneapolis, Minnesota, and practiced medicine for forty-two years. She began writing a memoir of her Holocaust experience in 1996, when she retired from a career in medicine. Zimering's *Hiding in the Open: A Holocaust Memoir* became a radio talking book for the blind and a stage play at a local history theater.

Henry Oertelt (Jewish) (b. 1920)

Henry Oertelt was born in Berlin. His family escaped the Nazis until 1943, when he was sent to a series of camps. Oertelt describes his survival of the Holocaust as a series of links in a chain; if one link had been broken, he would not have survived. These "links," he says, included the unexpected kindness from people and his being of small physical stature, having carpentry skills, and keeping an optimistic outlook, despite the grave conditions. Oertelt survived several death camps, including Auschwitz, and was finally liberated from Flossenburg while on a death march. Henry and his wife Inge live in Minnesota, where he has written his memoirs, *An Unbroken Chain: My Journey through the Nazi Holocaust.*

Oskar Schindler 1908–1974

An ethnic German, Schindler was born April 28, 1908, in Zwittau, Austria-Hungary (now Moravia in the Czech Republic). He was a businessman, and at first he saw the war as an opportunity to turn a profit by using Jewish slave labor in his factory. Later, however, he became more active in protecting his laborers. He helped thirteen hundred Jews from his factory survive deportations and extermination. Questions have arisen as to how much Schindler participated in protecting his workers, but as one Schindler Jew said, "I don't know what his motives were. . . . What's important is that he saved our lives." Schindler died in 1974, alone and penniless. In 1993, Jewish-American director Steven Spielberg turned a book about Schindler's life into the Oscar-winning film *Schindler's List* (1993).

Allies the nations, primarily Great Britain, France, the Soviet Union, and the United States, allied against the Axis powers, primarily Germany, Italy, and Japan, during World War II.

anti Semitism hatred of and discrimination against Jews.

Aryan in Nazi racial theory, a person of "pure" German "blood." The term "non-Aryan" was used to designate Jews, part-Jews, Gypsies, and others of supposedly "inferior" racial stock.

concentration camp a prison that holds prisoners without regard to accepted norms of arrest and detention.

death camp Nazi extermination center where Jews and other victims were killed as part of Hitler's "Final Solution."

death march forced march of prisoners over long distances and under intolerable conditions. Death marches were used by the Nazis to kill their victims.

deportation the act of expelling or banishing from a country or region people whose presence in that country or region is deemed unlawful.

displaced persons people who, during a war, have lost or been removed from their homes and have no where live.

Displaced Persons Act of 1948 law passed by U.S. Congress limiting the number of Jewish displaced persons who could emigrate to the United States.

dissidents people who disagree with a religious or political system or organization.

Einsatzgruppen mobile killing squads formed to follow the German army as it conquered land in eastern Europe and murder the Jews.

euthanasia also called mercy killing; painlessly killing or allowing the death of a person who is suffering a painful and/or incurable illness; Hitler's term for his program of killing disabled persons.

"Final Solution" a Nazi term used for the plan to exterminate the Jews of Europe.

führer German meaning "leader;" Adolf Hitler's title in Nazi Germany.

gas chambers large chambers in which people were executed by poisonous gas.

genocide the deliberate and systematic destruction of a racial, political, cultural, or religious group.

Gestapo acronym for *Geheime Staatzpolizei,* the "secret state police." The Gestapo was the intelligence wing of the *Sturmabteilung* and used brutal methods to investigate and suppress resistance to Nazi rule in Germany.

ghettos areas, usually established in the poor sections of a city, where most of the Jews from the city were forced to live. Ghettos were often surrounded by barbed wire or walls.

Gypsies a collective term for the Romani, a nomadic people believed to have come originally from northwest India and now living in Europe and other areas of the world.

Hitler Jugend (Hitler Youth) a Nazi youth group for teenaged boys established in 1926. After 1939, membership was compulsory in Germany.

Holocaust the systematic extermination of about six million European Jews by the Nazis.

International Military Tribunal a court established in August 1945 by the Allied powers of the United States, Great Britain, the Soviet Union, and France to prosecute major war criminals of the European Axis powers, mainly Italy and Germany.

Kristallnacht Night of Broken Glass. November 9, 1938—almost two hundred synagogues were destroyed, over eight thousand Jewish shops were ransacked and looted, and tens of thousands of Jews were removed to concentration camps.

lebensraum German meaning "living space;" a basic Nazi belief that more space was needed for Aryan Germans, compelling the Nazi invasion of European countries.

Majdanek Nazi camp and killing center opened in late 1941 near Lublin in eastern Poland.

Mein Kampf German meaning "my struggle;" the title of Hitler's book, published in 1925, which detailed his radical ideas of German nationalism, Aryanism, and anti-Semitism.

nationalistic having a great loyalty to one nation, exalting that nation above all other nations and promoting its culture and interests above all others.

The Nazi (National Socialist German Workers') Party political party founded in Germany on January 5, 1919; its platform was based on militaristic, racial, anti-Semitic, and nationalistic policies.

Nuremberg Race Laws laws announced by Hitler at the Nuremberg Nazi Party conference. These laws defined exactly who the Nazis would consider as Jewish and regulated the discrimination and persecution of Jewish people.

propaganda false or partly false information used to sway the opinions of a population.

Reichstag the German parliament under the Weimar Republic.

Schutzstaffel (SS or Protective Police) the SS formed in 1925 as Hitler's personal guard. Later under the control of Heinrich Himmler, the SS developed into the most powerful organization affiliated with the Nazi party.

shtetl a small Jewish town or village in eastern Europe.

Sobibór extermination camp located in the Lublin district of eastern Poland.

Sonderkommando Jewish slave labor units in extermination camps that removed the bodies of those gassed for cremation or burial.

sterilizations making humans or animals unable to reproduce. The Nazis performed sterilizations on people they deemed "inferior."

Sturmabteilung (SA, Storm Troopers, or "Brownshirts") the Nazi Party's military wing that persecuted Nazi opponents and facilitated Hitler's rise to and stay in power.

swastika a symbol used by early German nationalists to associate themselves with the Aryan race and later used by the Nazis as their emblem.

synagogue Jewish house of worship.

Treaty of Versailles a peace treaty signed by World War I victors and losers, including Germany, at the end of the war. The treaty forced Germany to accept responsibility for World War I.

Wannsee Conference Nazi conference held on January 20, 1942, on a lake near Berlin. At this conference, SS official Reinhard Heydrich helped present and coordinate the "Final Solution."

Weimar Republic the democratic government of Germany established after the end of World War I and lasting until 1933.

Zyklon-B (hydrogen cyanide) poisonous pesticide used in some gas chambers of Nazi death camps.

Please visit our web site at: www.garethstevens.com
For a free color catalog describing our list of high-quality
books, call 1-800-542-2595 or 1-800-387-3178 (Canada).

Library of Congress Cataloging-in-Publication Data

Bartel, Judy.
   The Holocaust: a primary source history / Judy Bartel.
      p. cm. — (In their own words)
   Includes bibliographical references and index.
   ISBN-13: 978-0-8368-5979-9 (lib. bdg.)
   ISBN-10: 0-8368-5979-0 (lib. bdg.)
   1. Holocaust, Jewish (1939-1945)—Juvenile literature. I. Title.
II. In their own words (Milwaukee, Wis.)
D804.34.B37   2005
940.53'18—dc22   2005046497

This North American edition first published in 2006 by
Gareth Stevens Publishing
A Weekly Reader® Company
1 Reader's Digest Road
Pleasantville, NY 10570-7000 USA

This U.S. edition copyright © 2006 by Gareth Stevens, Inc.
Original edition copyright © 2005 ticktock Entertainment Ltd.
First published in Great Britain in 2005 by ticktock Media Ltd.,
Unit 2, Orchard Business Centre, North Farm Road,
Tunbridge Wells, Kent, TN2 3XF, U.K.

Gareth Stevens editor: Carol Ryback

Gareth Stevens art direction: Tammy West
Gareth Stevens designer: Jenni Gaylord

Photo credits: (b=bottom; c=center; l=left; r=right; t=top)
Alamy: 6(b), 7(t), 18(b), 22(all), 23(t). Art Archive: 5(b), 8(b), 9(r), 19(cr),
32-33(all). CORBIS: 5(r), 7(b), 9(t), 10(b), 12(b), 13(b), 25(c), 16(cl),
27(all), 30-31(all), 35(t), 37(b), 38(all). Everett Collection: 35(b). United
States Holocaust Memorial Museum: 2, 24(b), 25(b), 16(t), 18l, 20(t),
20(b), 21(b), 23(cr), 26(all), 27(all), 36(b).

Every effort has been made to trace the copyright holders. We apologize
in advance for any unintentional omissions. We would be pleased to
insert the appropriate acknowledgments in any subsequent edition of
this publication.

Printed in the United States of America

2 3 4 5 6 7 8 9 10 09 08 07